ROBERT PRIEST

*To Yonah
Good Health
— [signature]
2006*

OTHER WORKS BY ROBERT PRIEST

Poetry
The Visible Man (Unfinished Monument Press)
Sadness of Spacemen (Dreadnaught)
The Man who broke out of the letter X (Coach House Press)
The Mad Hand (Coach House Press)
Scream Blue Living (The Mercury Press)

Sound Recordings
The Robert Priest E.P. (Airwave Records)
Rotweiller Pacifist (Coach House Press)
Tongue'n Groove (EMI-Artisan)

Selected Works for Children
The Short Hockey Career of Amazing Jany (Aya Press)
The Ruby Hat (Aya Press)
Daysongs Nightsongs (Groundwood Press)
Knights of the Endless Day (Penguin, Viking)
The Ballad of the Blue Bonnet (Groundwood Press)
A Terrible Case of the Stars (Penguin, Puffin)

Recordings
Summerlong: The Boinks
Lullabies & Playsongs: The TEDS
Winterlong: The TEDS

RESURRECTION IN THE CARTOON

Copyright © Robert Priest, 1997

All rights reserved. No part of this publication may be reproduced, stored in a retrieval system, or transmitted in any form by any process — electronic, mechanical, photocopying, recording, or otherwise — without the prior written permission of ECW PRESS.

Versions of some of these poems have appeared previously in *Exile, The Blue Penny Quarterly, Now, Dada Baby, Scream Blue Living* (New & Selected Poems), *Sadness of Spacemen, This Magazine, Rampike* and on *Friday Night* and *Imprint*.

Audio versions of some of these poems are available on Robert Priest's new CD *Tongue 'N Groove* (EMI/Artisan).

ECW PRESS

Canadian Cataloguing in Publication Data

Priest, Robert, 1951–
Resurrection in the cartoon

Poems.
ISBN 1-55022-313-5

I. Title.

PS8581.R47R47 1997   C811'.54   C96-932471-5
PR9199.3.P74R47 1997

Published with the assistance of The Canada Council and the Ontario Arts Council.

Back cover photo by Michael Jordan.
Design and imaging by ECW Type & Art, Oakville, Ontario.
Printed by Imprimerie Gagné, Louiseville, Québec.
Editor for the press: Michael Holmes.

Distributed in Canada by General Distribution Services, 30 Lesmill Road, Don Mills, Ontario M3B 2T6.

Visit Robert Priest's web-site at
www.interlog.com/~rpriest/index.htm

Published by ECW PRESS,
2120 Queen Street East, Suite 200,
Toronto, Ontario M4E 1E2.
www.ecw.ca/press

This book is dedicated to the memory of my grandmother Frances "Queenie" Wheatley, & my uncle, Charlie Slade

*Thanks to: My Beloved Marsha Kirzner,
Jim McNamara, Alannah Myles &
Nancy Simmonds, Mendelson Joe,
Michael Holmes, Huck & Mildred Kirzner,
and my parents Beatrice & Ted Priest.
The author also wishes to thank
The Ontario Arts Council, and especially the
Toronto Arts Council, for financial support
during the writing of some of these poems.*

*Also in memory of
Roger Slemin (thanks for Congo Toronto)
'Fuge'
Mary Hawkins
Colleen Petersen
& Elizabeth Smart*

RESURRECTION IN THE CARTOON

Priest.zip   13
Resurrection in the Cartoon   14
How to Swallow a Pig   16
Instructions for Laughter   18
The Stooge Iterations   19
The Stooge By-Laws   22
The Big Face Competition   23
The Three Disciple Stooges   24
My Three Stooges   25
The Three Sexual Survivor Stooges   26
Bladerunner Stooges   27
The Immortal Stooges   28
Friday Night   29
Ode to Distraction   30
Parallelvis Universes   31
The Presley Twins   35
You Call Me King   37
Elvis/Bacchus Iterations   38
Jesus and the Plus Sign   39
The Execution of Malnutrition   40
Death in the Cartoon   41
Blasphemy   42
The Non-Violent Boxer   43

WORDFARE

Little Right Wing Song Against the Victims   47
Money   48
Little Right Wing Victory Song   49
Ode to the Mother   50
Vote Shit   51
Modified Famous Phrases   52
How Much Patience   53
When You Call Someone Dickhead   54
Poem for the Ancient Trees   55
The Revenge Fuck   56

Injustice System 57
The Glasnost Iterations 58
Tired: A Little Right Wing Lullaby 59
The Coca-Cola Name-Change Song 60
The New Opportunity 63
Do Not Read This Poem 67
More Time Release Poems 68

IN SLOW APOCALYPSE

Messenger 73
Incarnation 74
Poem for Reluctant Thread 76
The Redress 77
Daniel Age 3 78
Prayer for My Son 79
Grandmother 80
Prayer for My Friends in Pain 82
Jack the Insomniac 83
Tracking Hands 85
Medium 86
Ode to the Asshole 87
Post-Modern Penis 89
About the Creation of Life on Earth 91
Our Spirits Are Trying to Get at One Another 93
Some Very Good Reasons Why 94
Safe Rage with Mates 95
There is No Silence 97
It is not Love at First Sight 98
Poem You Can't Refuse 99
In Slow Apocalypse 101
We Rode the Word 102
Women Looking Better Longer 103
This Life I'm Supposed . . . 105
Transformer 107
Fixing the Seed 109

*If it can't be laughed at
it shouldn't be in the Dao.*
　　　— Lao Tzu

RESURRECTION IN THE CARTOON

PRIEST.ZIP

OK pkunzip my brains now
I know these can't be words
unzip me to
my more elaborated angel state
unravel the real weaver
from inside me
give me self-extracting answers
please
initiate install install

RESURRECTION IN THE CARTOON

Here in the cartoon
resurrection is no miracle

Krishna, Christ, Lazarus
their risings are commonplace, profane
just a logical extension of the accident of death
usually humorous

The avatar cat rising up to face the cannon yet again
to be skinned once more by the escalator

There are no saviours in cartoons
no real redemption

Nor is there transformation
the duppy drawing springs back to life
always insanely intent
relentlessly pursuing
something quicker
smarter
than itself

And so we're dragged through the hoop
stripped down to some bone-self
the dumb button just jammed right in
automatic

The cruel karma machine
the wind-up cross, the electric man-hurler
I've come down on nails
on heads
on sticky stuff
an animated Hephaestus
still smelling of Aphrodite
still red with the raw hand of Zeus upon my back

I am hurled down repeatedly
a rubber Satan
a bouncy Christ
my features moving
so fast they distort
my feet on treadmill
my feet on insane

But I have power in the situation
I can run out over the edge of the cliff
and look — if I whirr my legs —
for seconds
I don't fall

HOW TO SWALLOW A PIG

Because of the shape of its face, a pig is actually one of the easiest animals to swallow whole.* Still, pig-swallowing is a very difficult and potentially dangerous activity. If you have advance notice, a certain amount of jaw-stretching and lip-widening prior to the event is always helpful. Your greatest enemy is self-doubt. You have to look at the pig's head and tell yourself that you *can* do this. Once you have greased the pig, begin by letting the fine tapered end of the snout proceed through your lips. The first obstacle, if it is not the back of your throat, will likely be your front teeth. Unfortunately these will have to be broken off. This clears the way for the full face-taper of the pig snout to zero in on your gullet. You have to be thinking "outrage" when this begins to happen for it is entirely violating and painful. But your throat can take it. Allow the gorge to widen as though it were a fluid, thinner with each stretch. You throat is a powerful python, infinitely elastic and accommodating. Once the entire pig head has squeezed by your gag reflex and entered your gorge you are fully committed. You will not be able to vomit out the pig safely. Nor can you wait long to continue, for at this time your trachea is entirely blocked by the pig's head. You are unable to breathe. Do not panic. Do not attempt to gasp or retch. Concentrate on swallowing. Having the wideness of the pig's bulky shoulders in your once narrow throat is perhaps the most violating thing you will ever experience. But you can do this. Just tell yourself: this is possible. Swallow and stretch. Keep your lower jaw loose to prevent the bone from snapping at the hinge. Suck with your guts. Use your lower diaphragm to draw the fat pig ever further down the gullet. Let your thick and lucent saliva lubricate the way. Saturating the pig with your juices will allow the celiated gorge to usher the pig deeper and deeper into your being. You may now need a friend with a stick to stuff in the pig's back end. This is the most crucial period. You will have been without oxygen for quite some time. You are probably blue in the face, but if you can widen to your most extreme limit, your throat cracking like wet bark, you will be able to slide your blue lips over the bare buttocks and with the last kick of the back trotters, the curl of the pig's tail will be gone. The entire pig is in your throat. Your intestines are stretching. Peristalsis has begun. The glottis is finally released and the first, terrible new breath can come with a gasp. You've lived! You've swallowed the whole pig. And now that it's entirely in your stomach you have to ask yourself: Is this not a most familiar feeling? Is this not the greatest feeling on earth?

*It is also one of the easiest animals to shove up the anus. This is not recommended for reasons of hygiene.

INSTRUCTIONS FOR LAUGHTER

It is not proper to go "HA! HA!", open-mouthed, squinty-eyed, pointing. Laughing can be executed with perfect grace, elegance, and still be 100 per cent expressive. Laugh with a straight spine. Let the kundalini energy come straight up and have its own little dance in the beauty of your face. Don't use laughing to shiver out disgust at your world, your self, whatever lies are coiling too tight that night. Don't use laughter to sneak some grief out. Don't make hollow "Aaaw Aaaaaw" or "Eeee-Eeee" sounds just to rattle some subterranean bit of the unused muscle of love. Don't stuff your laugh with terror bits. Don't push up a ragged laugh at outrage or half-turn a laugh that ends in shock or shame. Don't laugh in a high voice like a puppy when you don't mean it. A laugh is not a bag you carry out the psychic trash in. You must not laden it with death-dread and toxic, boxy bits of brokenness. Let your body be a tickled trumpet-tit to the laughter. Let the giddy laughter play you like a tongue in the heart till you're undone. Laugh till your genitalia are laughing too. Let each vein mouth laugh. But do not brazenly bend over with your hands on your knees and scream. Real laughter can occur at volumes well below 12-14 db. It is uncommon for evolved laughter to continue into weeping, but this on occasion can and does occur. In such instances it is proper to wipe tears only with one hand — the funny hand. (Decide which hand is funniest and let it wipe the tears.) It is considered vulgar to seek out laughter. It must come in the accidental course of living. Only this is true laughter. And so it is not proper to attend so-called comedy clubs, church services, or any reading, anywhere, of sacred vows.

THE STOOGE ITERATIONS:
REPORT ON ACTIVITIES OF "THREE STOOGES"

CURLY'S REPORT

I could never speak about it before because nothing had ever been said to make me think anything positive could come of it. So I would try to make it funny and people actually laughed. But Moe was really hitting me. He was poking me in the eyes. He was twisting my ear right round in circles and everybody just watched and laughed. Is the horrifying hollow clunk of one head colliding with another funny, even if you go "wu"? I should have let my needs be known. I should have said: "This isn't funny — I'm hurting!" But I couldn't speak. And Moe was kicking me hard a lot of the time — kicking me in the coccyx or tugging on my tongue. And when I wasn't tensing up against the next onslaught, I was watching poor sweet Larry getting his hair torn out in fist-fulls that sounded like sheets of cotton ripping. The poor bastard — poked, seared, scalded, torn. Sure I hated Moe — more than anything. And yes, it's true, whether deliberately or not I still don't know, 'cause I may have just convinced myself it was an accident, but one day Moe got his head completely stuck in a stovepipe and me and Larry decided we were gonna "help" him, so, well, we put our feet on his shoulders and pulled at the stovepipe as hard as we both could. After a while — when he stopped screaming in there, all you heard were these "pingy" sounds of his neck bones popping and we knew we could just tug his head right off if we wanted. But we stopped and tried to twist the stovepipe off instead. Once again he gasped and cried out but we just went right on with both hands, turning that stovepipe round and round 'til his nose bone crunched and steam shot out. But those day are gone now. People thought it was funny, so we went along with it. Now we pay. And that's just the way it is.

WITNESS' REPORT

Well the little one — Moe — the nasty one — when he found out what had happened, he got so enraged, he deliberately poked two fingers right into Curly's eyes. I've never seen a man poked in the eyes before and I was quite shocked. Curly, in agony, pulled both palms down over his face to his chin, one hand after the other, in rapid succession, all the while emitting an agonized kind of "wub-wub-wub-wub" sound, high in register — dog-like in intensity. I watched helplessly as the same arm which had so cruelly poked the fingers into Curly's eyes shot back, the elbow high, right onto the bridge of Larry's nose. This caused Larry to do something which deeply disturbed me. Taking the huge monkey wrench he had been holding, he somehow managed to spike its grips up Moe's nostrils and with some quick turns, tighten it to grip the septum. To my horror, while Curly inscribed a heel-driven circle on the floor and continued his heart rending "wub-wub-wubs," Larry then proceeded to twist Moe's nose completely around on his face until the cartilage yielded a sharp "pop." Unable to move, Moe began to run on the spot, going "Nya-aaa-aaaa!" in agony.

WITNESS' REPORT II

Perhaps the most horrifying part of it all, though, is the terrible and unexpected sounds human body parts make as they are yanked, disconnected, and pierced. For, unlike the muffled underflesh retorts we would expect from snapping femurs and popping joints, we get highly oscillating "Proing!" type sounds more reminiscent of the mechanical world — springs, gaskets, etc. Human flesh, when whacked, sounds much more like wood than water for instance, and there are apparently notches in the neck that creak in precise increments when corkscrewed — Nok! Nok! Nok! — 'til the face comes right back round again, ready to be let go — Proing! And these are only a few of the many violent and repetitively brutal, even handicapping acts which I saw these three men perform during my three-week stay. The surprising thing to me though, was the speed at which they reconciled. After repeated brutal assaults they could apparently, without ceremony or apology, completely forgive, forget, and get along with one another. (If only to perform one more foolish, useless task.) More than their own violence, however, was called into play. They had an enormous propensity for attracting and eliciting aggression from those around them. Perhaps the most humiliating thing that can be done to a human being is to shove a cream pie in his or her face. When such an attack occurs in a room full of people and pies, these three men have a strange catalyzing, chain reaction effect on even the most distinguished guests. One can barely watch when all, finally, give way — the good and the bad, the handsome and the sad — to this profoundly humiliating urge — to throw a pie. To see heads jerked back by pies, heads shoved down, suffocatingly deep into pies. To see pies splat two, three people at a time. To see people shoved head first into wedding cakes, and vast vats of icing dumped on heaps of rioting people. To watch helplessly as faces, nostril-flared, are forced into foam and cherry and sense the almost ecstatic quality of these actions is a profoundly disturbing and ultimately unsettling experience which ought not to be witnessed by the faint of heart.

THE STOOGE BY-LAWS

It is illegal to poke a stooge in the eyes
Falling to the floor and running in a sideways circle is
 prohibited
There will be no hair pulling in the common room
Please do not bring pliers into these premises
It is forbidden — while running on the spot super
 fast — to exhale steam from the nostrils
There will be absolutely no pulling out of chunks of hair
No excoriating the eyes
It is wrong to punch the lungs out

Anyone caught laughing at violent acts will be expelled
Until further notice all pies are strictly forbidden in the
 cafeteria area
It is a crime to seat a stooge in a catapult
A stooge may not give final unction
No electrocuting stooges
Anyone caught hanging a stooge will be suspended

THE BIG FACE COMPETITION

The winners of the big face competition
are awarded face enlargements
by serious plastic surgeons

Afterward they are promoted to the B grant category
and put up against other former winners

There are no juries for these events
as the size of a face is an absolute
and determinable quantity

Everything from the tip of the nose
to the inner back lobe of the ear
is considered face
and remember it is surface that counts

Measurement is attained
by immersion in a tub or vat of lard

For application in other areas or disciplines
please contact Henri Offender
or his
little
knave

THE THREE DISCIPLE STOOGES

Curiously, the only censored version of the Stooges is the rarely screened *The Three Stooges in Galilee*. This episode is rumoured to show Curly in Jerusalem, spending an entire day stealing fish from various merchants. Larry, elsewhere, pilfers loaf after loaf of bread from all the bakeries. Moe, meanwhile, has ingested a magic mushroom of some kind while scarfing the Messiah's abandoned stew. As he stands on the table extemporizing to the gathered masses on lilies and things, Curly and Larry successfully deliver, beneath the table, the loaves and fishes. The miracle is ready.

After the sermon, when the bakers and the fishmongers see the banquet that has been prepared for them, they recognize their pilfered wares and rise up to crucify all three.

MY THREE STOOGES

In the equally rare *My Three Stooges* Moe is a father and Curly and Larry are little kids. AND HE STILL BEATS THEM! In these episodes it's not dames that Curly's always after — it's Mom. Moe, as in all versions of the Stooges, repeatedly pops both children in the eyes. The sonic effects, however, have been altered. They are squelchier now. A little painful to hear but still possibly funny. Arse kicks have a little coccyx crack-and-crunch undertone; while the two-in-a-line, double child-face-slap is actually the sound of a wet seal being fwapped by fishermen on a marble floor TWICE! Curly and Larry have learned to laugh a lot of the physical stuff off. They are geniuses at turning their shock, the deep sense of betrayal, into big, camera-hogging hams that are truly hilarious. These are great child actors! Because it's the old days we are not allowed to actually see Moe when he thrashes their asses. He takes them in a room off-camera. And the kids are great. They're trembling great. There's water in their veins. Their bowels are going. Moe is going to beat them.

The next time we see them their asses are in buckets and there is steam rising off of them. They have obviously been crying. Curly, even though his voice is hoarse from screaming, manages the first mock "Nyaah ahah," making Larry pull his goo face. During the filming of this series, Curly Howard, the actor who plays Curly, succumbs to a stroke and is unable to perform. But Curly is replaced by older brother Shemp. Shemp dies, also of a stroke. The final Stooge is Joe Besser. Joe takes on the moniker Curly Joe, and keeps the part until the show is cancelled due to poor ratings.

THE THREE SEXUAL SURVIVOR STOOGES

In a bizarre twist, we have now uncovered a case of sexual Stooge abuse. AND IT'S STILL FUNNY. In this series, instead of poking Curly in the eyes, the aptly named Moe gives him rapid pokes up the asshole. Larry suffers repeated penis yanks, twists, scrunches, whacks, and hammers. All with extremely unexpected sonic repercussions. DOING! DWANG! FLOOMPF! Larry's penis is cut, burnt, yanked or twisted off an average of 7 times an episode. Fortunately for Larry, his penis seems to have more regenerative properties than Wolverine. Ever-reborn and newly sensitive, Larry is an immortal abuse victim. AND IT'S STILL FUNNY.

In the episode with the elephant, Curly, Larry and Moe have all been locked, bare-bummed, into stocks. When the elephant sees the large pot of vaseline it fucks each of the Stooges with a big, popping, tearing sound. Moe as usual moans "NYAAAA AAAAAH!", while Curly goes "WOOO WOOOO WOOOO." AND IT'S STILL FUNNY!

BLADERUNNER STOOGES

In this episode, Moe is an android doomed to die. His hair has only just started to fall out. It is a young Moe, more handsome than we would have thought possible. He has seen the cargo ships on fire off Orion. He has seen things you've never dreamed, but now, at his peak, he must die. It's part of his programming — unless he can find Curly and Larry. Curly and Larry invented Moe. And a million more Moes. Moes everywhere all over the stars like little lumberjacks building the brick shit-house of interstellar commerce and the marketplace. And what if some of these android Moes should get ambitious or go crazy? Well that's why they had the built-in time limit thing. It was written into the materials of their genesis. It *is* them — this early death. How Moe hates it. How enraged he is at these little men who have made him. Who are less than him. In the end he finds Curly and Larry but they assure him haughtily that he is untreatable. They make offensive platitude-like remarks drawn largely from self-help books they have only just read and therefore believe. Moe says, "Pick two fingers." Curly stupidly complies and Moe rapidly pokes them in Curly's sockets, deep past the eyeballs, into the soft brain stuff behind — until the too-red blood runs out. Then he turns to Larry and says, "Pick two fingers."

THE IMMORTAL STOOGES

Due to some Satanic deals, no-one at this particular banquet can actually be killed. They can, however, be maimed, exploded, and pierced. So Moe pulls out the double-barrelled twelve gauge shotgun and says, "Hey Larry — take a look in the binoculars." Moe's gone a bit far this time. He lets Larry have it, full blast in both eyes, basically disintegrating the top two-thirds of Larry's head — some of the slushy pink stuff still caught, hanging from the remaining hair — flip-top-box-like. Larry, unable to see, lets Moe have it in the guts. Unfortunately it's not Moe. It's the fat diplomat who has just bent down to bow to the finicky lady. This gentleman is outraged when his buttocks are blasted open. En masse, his seven sons open fire on the Stooges. Unfortunately they are terrible marksmen. Curly is going "woo woo" as fast as possible. He has been sped up or something. He has transformed the gunshots into bells and buzzers as he deeks and ducks, still expertly pulling faces. Moe, however, is being rammed again and again against the blood-spattered walls as he is repeatedly shot by the brothers. Each time he rises back up more and more raggedly. Unfortunately so does the small boy who has been putting glass in the punch. So does the overly dignified lady in the green lamé gown. Now several comedians pull out really big hand cannons and, laughing wildly, begin to blow away as many heads as possible, exploding them like watermelons. Guns are coming out everywhere: exploded, wounded, immortal people are shooting wildly, everyone's being drawn in. The whole place is just strings of guts and guns, implacably engaged in hatred and rage. Only Curly still dodges the inaccurates. Only Curly: immaculate, unkillable, and still funny.

FRIDAY NIGHT

(Old English: fri — free. Germanic: freond — friend, lover. Belonging to the beloved.)

It's the tin can top of the week you rip off ragged
and suddenly the streets are bowels, sluice gates
squirming with workees, herdies, suits let loose.
Yes, it's time to hunt the huntress
or have the huntress hunt you.
'Cause tonight you get to do what you wanna do. Free.
Because there's something in the net again.
Maybe a wish,
maybe a cod fish,
maybe a ballot or a bullet
but there's something in the net.

Even if you've been refused before.
Even if you've cowered for ten generations
in iron obedience, just plug-in to whatever is a socket
and receive, 'cause this is the night
when the pekineeze pops from the pea pod
and we are knee-deep in dancing dogs.
It's a night to crank open
a couple cartons of condoms
and have safe sex 24 times.

Wheel up your fleet of easy chairs and stare awhile.
By order of the state it's an outrage,
it's you it's the beloved,

it's Friday night.

ODE TO DISTRACTION

hail distraction
glittering distraction
shallow glossy distraction
that keeps my mind out of the wound
that keeps my consciousness out of the red trough
all praise to those who make
the shitty music of our times
blessed be the sitcom writers
thank god for muzak from which i made $2.67
for muzak which suckles me
off the outrageous silence in elevators
thank you thank you admen
promo makers, puffers of blowers
thank you sign makers, and *Pepsi*
for keeping me off the landscape
praise be the makers of tryptophan so that i sleep
i am grateful for *People* magazine
thanks not only for news
but for news about newsmen —
how they are doing
retrospectives on them
i do not want always to stare
at the bloody brutal beauty
all around me naturally
let there be answers
let there be logic to it all
praise the astronaut and those
who'd get us off earth physically
praise the gods
of all religions and cartoons
i do not always want to lead my mind
down to the bloodied black waters
of truth

PARALLELVIS UNIVERSES

THE DEATH OF ELVIS 1

Elvis sat down on the toilet as big as Buddha and waited
it was the anniversary of his mother's death.
Elvis strained and his face went a little red
he thought of his mother dying that day
he had lost certain rights
he had become mythic in the mind
you lose so much when that happens.
Elvis strained again. He could feel something
moving in his centre.
Something really big.
Excited he pushed harder.
He pushed and grunted.
It was coming! It was coming!
Elvis strained until the purple veins stood out like
tree roots in his beet red neck
and then it came
bigger than Mt. Sinai it came
bigger than the first orgasm
like a deathstar spiral
the big black bolt shot through him
and Elvis keeled over
and groaned
a big fat man on the toilet
the sound of that last fart still reverberating
amidst the gasping
the crying
like any man dying.

ALTERNATE ELVIS REALITY A:)

Hideously disfigured
but at last anonymous again
Elvis
swept

ALTERNATE ELVIS REALITY B:)

Really happy about his new cunt
with the slow daily swelling of his new breasts
Elvis began to feel a fullness in his belly
such as he had never known
as a man

THE DEATH OF ELVIS 2

they went to get Jimmy Hoffa
but they got Elvis by mistake
that great voice wasted on the hook
that great vibrato ended with a boot to the throat
"I'm not Jimmy Hoffa!"
"I'm not Jimmy Hoffa!"

THE DEATH OF ELVIS 3

("They call it Elvis-lution" — Mojo Nixon)

Surprisingly limber on his small toes, at home,
in private, naked and very large, Elvis would dance.
There was no regret in his mind. He accepted each
new roll of fat with Buddhic glee.
It was not the svelte postal stamp Elvis that he loved.
He loved this new transformed Elvis.
An Elvis who had let a lot of stuff go —
handsomeness —
GULP! GULP! — gone, bloated, distorted,
that leer now, that sexual sneer just
a weird bit in the balloon that makes one whole
side of the face pull down in a slab askew.
But he cares not
for Elvis knows himself
he understands his soul-urge
and like a genius at home he can slink out
of his image-skin and be the man he is,
giggling and jiggling with fat.
Like a young Santa Claus, Elvis
sits and rolls his rolls and laughs.
He plays his great hits and twitches
mocking his old self with lewd
self-accepting rudenesses.
Carnal Elvis. The evolved Elvis.
Able to leap quite high now and spin in the air,
the big slap of those feet
as he lands ecstatic, sumo-like.
And Elvis is approaching the bathroom.
Yes, Elvis is approaching the bathroom.
It is the anniversary of his mother's death
and Elvis avatar is jumping and spinning wildly.
He has completely forgotten that he is Elvis Presley.
He is just a timeless bit of himself
soaring out towards the fated room

and alas, what might have been
if he had not just then landed
that delicate white foot on a bar of soap
and been upended, flipped over backwards. Smack!
Flop! On his great big belly
hard enough to bounce him halfway back up
and curiously, arse-first onto the toilet.
Already unconscious, the god-like head whips against
the supports of a shelf containing
ten round tins of spam.
These come rolling down one by one onto his head
until with a final THUNK!
the king is capsized from his throne,
already dead
onto the bathroom floor.

THE PRESLEY TWINS

It is widely known that Elvis was a twin. Official documents tell us that Elvis' identical twin brother Caan died at birth. But baby Caan never really died. There were always two Presley boys. When one appeared the other disappeared. When one emerged the other hid. Mrs. Presley liked it that way. A kid in the closet and a kid on TV. Usually, it was Caan who was kept in the closet; but when Caan came out Elvis went in, and that's how it was from day one for God had sent the two down and no-one else knew but Vernon and Lou. And Elvis had the raspy voice — the one that sang *Jailhouse Rock*, the one that sang *Hound Dog* — that hack-saw thing in the throat. Then he would leave the stage and Caan would come on and do the *Love Me Tenders*, the *Don't Be Cruels* in a sweet milky voice and no one knew. No one knew but Vernon and Lou and no one ever suspected. But after the fame came Caan started to want to come out of the closet but mother wouldn't allow it. There were threats, scenes. The brothers started fighting. Then, when he was drafted, it was Elvis who did all the time while Caan slacked off. This was when Caan started doing prescription drugs — all the pharmaceuticals he could get his hands on. You see Lou was the Doc and the Doc knew, and he thought he was prescribing for two but Caan was scarfing the lot. The twins began to look different. That is why, after the army, Caan and Elvis did so little TV.

There is a moment in the Elvis *Live from Hawaii* video, though, that is very telling. You think it's live and uncut but those who saw the original remember "Elvis," after sleezing his way through *Love Me Tender*, asking to be excused. He gets up laughing and leaves the whole world hanging for 4 minutes as he goes to the washroom. What is now evident is that the real Elvis was in there wearing an identical outfit. He came out and did that great hacksaw vocal on *One Night With You*. This is Elvis at his best. He can't stop smiling. There is no self-deprecation now. But notice his right hand — the familiar knuckle duster is no longer present — one of the few times any small detail of the elaborate substitution becomes detectable on camera. After that there began to be more and more physical differences between the two men. Sometimes Elvis would start a gig, thin, confident, then Caan would do the second night, already starting to bulge. The cheap American pharmaceuticals had begun to break down his capillaries. Elvis withdrew and watched helplessly from the sidelines as his brother slipped into the puffy, pathetic narcosis of the famed last days. That man who died on the toilet that day — his body should never have been found. He was to have been discreetly buried, out of the way finally, so that Elvis the survivor, might emerge at last — miraculously thin, confident, pelvic and laughing, to conduct the greatest comeback of all time. But the body was found. And to all the world this was Elvis. Stricken with the loss of his brother, the real Elvis saw his chance at freedom. Without telling a soul he headed for the nearest shopping plaza. And that is why there are so many sightings. Do you really think that many people could be wrong? It is Elvis that they are seeing. He is out there. Still.

YOU CALL ME KING

you call me king
you call me king
come see me on my throne then
come see my last judgement
come see my drugged noble lips slobber
in the death grin
i release it
i release it
a hardwire grin of mu metal
a metal that should
never be bent
or melted
or parted
a mouth not to be kissed
a hacksaw thing
a child thing
that used to sing so well
you call me king
you call me king

ELVIS/BACCHUS ITERATIONS

Elvis Bacchus, Elvis Bacchus
has no one else noticed the similarity
between these two names?
Say Bacchus 22 times using those precedents
of consonant decay over time
(as described by archaeologist
Colin Renfrew)
and Bacchus *is* Elvis.

Listen:

Bacchus Bacchus Bacus Bakis Bekis
Mekis Mawkiss Nawkis Nawbis Nawlbis
Nelbish Nelfish Snelfish Stelfish
cellfish elfish elfis — Elvis!

Elvis is Bacchus
Elvis in his prime
and Elvis in his decline
dead on the crapper
with a body full of drugs
Elvis is Bacchus
and Bacchus is us.

JESUS AND THE PLUS SIGN

Pontius Pilate said, "Jesus, you are too positive. You push everything towards affirmation, falling never into negativity. You add to the world your gallant and wise soul. You add to the environment your healing walk, your caress of the waters, and to humanity you add some sense of divinity in the flesh, some meaning, some worth. Too damn positive. Add. Add. After I wash my hands and clean my teeth you must carry a huge plus sign up Golgotha so that you can come to know the over-bearing mass of your positivity on the great Mathematics of Rome."

THE EXECUTION OF MALNUTRITION

They took Malnutrition out. They put it up against a wall and shot it. A billion bullets as it bucked and jolted, taking on a different shape with each blast — bird, star, stone, old man, woman, child, child, child. They riddled Malnutrition remorselessly but there was no killing it. Not the fire, not disease, not the explosion of hunger, not the haunted faces of billons could end its life. Malnutrition just took them on and stood there wide-eyed and staring, its long overdue ticket to the banquet — its death warrant — still clutched in its infant fist.

DEATH IN THE CARTOON

curiously
whenever a cartoon
is really
dead
beyond any further brutal
resurrection
this state
does not become final
until two crosses
appear
in the character's
eyes

BLASPHEMY

a cross chases you
a cruise cross
with automatic piercers
you run over wriggling landscapes
of mal-joined human limbs
as the cross soars
or hovers
coming closer
slanting its way through
narrow openings
or butting with its arms
to break through
the cross chases you
with portable Golgotha
and like everyone
you are screaming

"the only blasphemy
is violence"

THE NON-VIOLENT BOXER

He came from nowhere. The quickest ducker in the world. The fastest chin in existence. The non-violent boxer, just deeking and dodging, while his opponent flails away. *Thwip! Thwip!* Look at that guy move! Look at the way he pops that lightbulb-like head straight down, almost as though into some turtle hole in the top of his torso. Shhzooopp! And a fist cuts through naked air, the little guy's legs shooting wide apart. Five rounds and he hasn't been touched.

If you listen you can hear him over the ring mike trying to persuade his opponent. "Do you think it would be a victory if you beat me?" *Thwip!* "That would be just one more loss for both of us." *Thwip! Thwip!* "The greatest victory of all is in our grasp, but I need you my brother." *Thwip! Thwip! Thwip! Thwip! Thwip!*

WORDFARE

LITTLE RIGHT WING SONG AGAINST THE VICTIMS

For too long we have blamed the crime
on the perpetrator

It's time to get the victims
in their bloody bandage disguises
they hide magnets in their throats
manipulating with their exploded hearts
the great issues of the world

Behind every great savagery I assure you
lies the hand of the victim
perpetually burning, sinister with portent
the victim conducts human electricity
forking it ever to the crime

the skinny excuse of being mangled
the great alibi that they are too young
the mere technicality that they have been silenced

MONEY

All the dirt on money clean off onto your headstone
and coins with faces worn down by a million palms
nothing on it but the polyglot fingerprint —
the big thumb of nerves beneath which we all cower

All the dirt on money clean off into a lake
the great glacial eye rotating on its skein of sights
uncovers quicksilver creeping in the hatchery
the death rattle of Iroquois and salmon

All the filth and nervousness of money
contracted in a handshake
the great golden jingle that sucks out the water
and dirties it
little mirrors jingling with my king-face
and beasts extinct

All the breath breathed in want of money
all the deeds done for money
this round catalogue of agonies and consumption
this devouring head
o amulets ceaselessly fingered
o economy

LITTLE RIGHT WING VICTORY SONG:
THE WORKFARE PYRAMIDS (Ontario /97)

Single Mothers on Workfare pulling ploughs
Single Mothers on Workfare as a kind of 'living fence'
at the opera and at big shows like *Phantom*
and *Beauty and the Beast*
Single Mothers on Workfare
cleaning 2nd cars
in two-car families
Single Mothers on Workfare instead of streetlights
instead of alarm clocks,
instead of hat racks
Single Mothers on Workfare herding the cloned sheep
amalgamating oranges
buffing the gallows 2 hrs a day minimum
Single Mothers on Workfare
rowing galleys, making pyramids
Single Mothers on Workfare digging graves
looking after other people's kids
instead of their own

ODE TO THE MOTHER

Well into overtime
just as big men go down
and start to sleep
well into overtime
cry by cry
the great mother who made the men
who made the pyramids.
The mighty mother who birthed
and loved all the armies
and the generals and the dreamers.
This mightiest worker of them all.
For she is the support system
for the immobile and hungry infant
the government, the factory
the skyscraper of children.
She is the organizer and manager
of hostile properties
co-ordinator of juggled jobs
always on call, always going full tilt
too hard worked to lobby
for better wages
the work meaning more, trapped in the work
doing the work like Atlas, like Sheba
like Mother Theresa's mother.

I have a new perspective
on my respect for those who build stadiums
for those who gouge coal
from the bottom of the earth.

Let the steelworkers of legend
lay down their molten ingots
and take up for a while
a warm needing baby.

VOTE SHIT

It's just a big dogshit
someone left smiling
at the sky
but vote for this piece of shit.
Because it is the only socialist.
Because there is 7 per cent compassion in shit
and that makes shit tops.
Because you get a nice photo
of a piece of shit in a suit and tie
and shit looks good.
But shit is different.
Shit won't lie.
It's just some species of feces
but it will not cut social programs.
It won't offer the gag to the weakest in their screaming
as it cuts their throats
for all of us.
We are gonna keep conscience with shit.
Because shit can do it.
Because we deserve shit.
Because shit is what you want
when you don't know what it is
you really want.

MODIFIED FAMOUS PHRASES*
(or: *Butcher Slogans not People!*)

If we can put a man on the moon then
STOP THE WAR ON THE POOR

If wishes were horses, beggars would
STOP THE WAR ON THE POOR

Don't pick your nose or your eyes will
STOP THE WAR ON THE POOR

Spare the rod and
STOP THE WAR ON THE POOR

It takes a lot to laugh but it takes a train to
STOP THE WAR ON THE POOR

Forgive and
STOP THE WAR ON THE POOR

To gain the world and
STOP THE WAR ON THE POOR

I liked this new stainless steel blade so much
I had to go out and
STOP THE WAR ON THE POOR

*This poem is intended for use at demonstrations. The leader would call out the beginning of the famous phrase and the others would respond with the modified ending. Other famous phrases could be added, of course, and there might be many more modified endings, such as "Stop ailments!" or "Free Ontario!"

HOW MUCH PATIENCE

how much patience does it take
to wait forever
and still get nothing
how much virtue in that
how many forms before you get the final
form letter of denial
a blank wall
uncrossable
like a chasm

how much patience does it take
when you are hungry
when you are angry inside
when you are going crazy
how much does it take
to finally get
the same old answer
as before

somewhere someone has got you by your children
got you by your organs
got you by the blood you need
or just plain food to eat
and you know clearly what must be done

how much patience does it take
to lie there bleeding
and watch it
not get done

WHEN YOU CALL SOMEONE DICKHEAD

When you call someone Dickhead
you refer to the glans penis — the frenulum
the super sensitive male penis tip
an almost supernatural part of the anatomy
almost a brain
almost another hanging heart

When you call someone Dickhead
you insult the wizened face
of who knows what hung
ancestor
in this vivid
wrinkle
this lifeboat
on the big tug

When you say Dickhead
drop the inverse reverence
you are bestowing a well-earned title
this grandest of all grandissments
should be reserved for those whom
we respect the most
Popes, Premiers, heavy metal singers —
are Dickheads
because we are fair
because we respect the penis

POEM FOR THE ANCIENT TREES

I am young and
want to live
to be old
and I don't want to
outlive these trees —
this forest

When my last song is gone
I want these same trees
to be singing on —
newer green songs
for generations to come
so let me be old
let me grow to be ancient
to come as an elder
before these same temple-green sentinels
with my aged limbs
and still know a wonder that will outlast me
I want long love
long life
give me 150 years of good luck
but don't let me outlive these trees

THE REVENGE FUCK

we chose him for what he was not
we chose him for maximum hurtage
we chose him in anger
and on a whim
and now
we're stuck with him
the revenge fuck
who stayed
the revenge fuck
who takes over the house
for five years

there is some law that says
once you choose the revenge fuck
you have to get fucked
for five years straight
but we just wanted a quick fix
we just wanted a moment of balance
if we'd known
one taste of him
we would have puked
but now we live in glass houses
our children are afraid
and the whole place is run
by the revenge fuck
who stayed

INJUSTICE SYSTEM

when the killers have all been killed
when all the starvers have been starved
after the slaughter of the murderers
when the poisoners have all been poisoned
when the batterers have been battered right down
where they can't even stand
and the machete wielders have been slashed open
when the rapist has been raped and raped and raped
and the child beater has been beaten like a child
after we hang the last hang man
then i will bury the last of the grave-diggers
then i will judge the judges

THE GLASNOST ITERATIONS

Glasnost
Glasnost
Glaszjnoss
glassnnosn
glazznish
glassness
glawzniss
klashness
klowzniss
klowsnis
kloshness
klostness
closdness
closedness

TIRED: A LITTLE RIGHT WING LULLABY

i have been slitting the throats of lambs all day
i have been trying to galvanize public opinion
  against the poor
it is wearying sending so many women back to the
  suttee
i must rest my limbs from the strain
of denying benefits all day to single mothers, to the sick
i have been moving the possessions of ragged old men
  from rooms
taking away televisions from the paralyzed
and my back creaks with fatigue
i need some time to relax my hands
after a hard day strangling
a terrible day of execution after execution
till the trigger finger
is but a hook
i will need a rest from this day in and day out
hammering back the trumpets into twisted brass
smashing the flutes
i am so weary i don't think i could sentence
one more young black man
i haven't the energy left to beat a single child

i feel like i could sleep forever

THE COCA-COLA NAME-CHANGE SONG

Coca-Cola
aka Coke
you share your name with
the continental bogy drug
cocaine
aka coke

in fact you used to use cocaine
in your actual secret brew
Coke
but when the law changed, you changed too
the right thing to do
but you kept the name — Coke
and you sell the name, Coke, big time
all around the world

Coke is it
Coke is it

so how does that read to the mind of
the close-to-first-time drug user
about to maybe slip into a lifetime of addiction

Coke is it
Coke is it

on all the little treadmills of potential anaesthesia

Coke is it
Coke is it

you sell coke, Coke
and when you sell Coke
the soft drink,
you sell coke
the hard drug
you sell both
you sell Coke
and you sell coke

there's Coke the pop
and coke you pop into your veins
oh Coke Coke
you have a moral responsibility here
to change your name
to change
your name

2. SOME NEW NAMES FOR COKE

Folka-Cola — Good Aryan hook. Plus it recalls 'folk' music — big with the kids. Subliminally the 'fuck' in folk is good: "We're Foke — the cola that dares to change its name."

Polka-Cola — Great East European dance groove. Plus the 'poke' in Polka will hook in nicely with the well-established 'look at this big foaming dick' techniques already so well exploited.

Tolka-Cola — This offers subliminally the alternative to cocaine of a good safe herbal remedy.

Christa-Cola — So they can push the state religion and Coke too. *Christ is it!*

THE NEW OPPORTUNITY

This poem is not brought to you by Molson's
but it was close believe me.
You see I had just done days of visualizations
asking for new opportunities
doing a vigil like a new Knight
for this latest fad of cutbacks
when the phone rings
and its someone from an ad company
and they are doing a kind of
"spoken word" thing for Molson's.
It will be subtle. It will be a poem.
And at the end there'll just be a little
"presented by Molson's" kind of thing.
"A poem?"
"A poem," they say.
"And the client is asking specifically for you
but you *will* have to audition."
"No. I don't do that sort of thing," I tell them.
"How much is it?"

It turns out to be a couple of grand
and maybe its the beginning of a series of commercials
and if I'm the voice for all of them
then we're talking more like 8000 bucks.
Hmmm. 8000 bucks. And I've been asking the universe
for new opportunities. I'm being tested. I can tell.
My stomach is clenched.
So, what to do?

I have a family to support.
I haven't had a B grant for seven years.
I haven't had a works-in-progress grant for seven years.
I've been living off the income from a song
and the income has dwindled down to oh so little
just as the ultra right has taken over the government

cutting grants and worse yet, cutting welfare
and introducing workfare.
8 grand over time is looking good.

All the next day I agonize.
I like beer — Upper Canada beer — not Molson's swill.
But I won't actually be advertising said beer
I will merely be reciting some crap pseudo poem.
I am being tested by the gods.
But which way to go?

Every moment of the day hovers
over which way I'll take this.
How will it be to hear my voice
emerge from passing cars
betraying itself a 1000 times an hour
all over the nation —
this voice I've kept so pure.

And what if others recognize it?
What if Poet B hears it?
Poet C would surely hold me in utter contempt
for this one slip-up.
Worst of all there's outright
outside revolutionary poet@.com.
Is my reputation worth only a shot at 8 grand?
That's not even half a B grant!
"All you're doing is acting."
But the voice itself is sacred.
No, matter is profane!
It is a test to see if you are in the world.
This is the way the dirty world moves
and you are part of the mud
and the muck and the swill of the world
and you have a family to support.

I'm almost at the sound studio now
but it could still go either way.

I could easily get off the streetcar
at the next stop and just not show up.
In fact I'm now half an hour late. Good.
Even if I do show up (I've entered the building now)
at least I've shown some disrespect.

Fuck the world anyway
for making times so hard for a poet.
This is what you get.
Daintily now I'm approaching
Comfort Sound Studios.
I'm striding down a long hallway
to a door off the side at the end.
There is the sound of chatter from inside.
A smell of tobacco.
I am nervous like a man about to make a speech —
like someone who is going to be whipped.
I round the last corner
and there in the waiting room
are some people I know.
Why its poets B & C.
Plus other poets.
Poets I have never met.
Poets I have always wanted to meet.
Young poets.
Old poets.
I look around and even poet@.com is there.
One guy looks sheepish
others brazen unashamed
most merely matter of fact
resigned.

After we all recite the pseudo poem
written by an adman
Poet H
and I retreat to a local coffee shop
where he tells me he is
the new poetry editor for a certain press.

He wonders if he can have a look at my next book.
This book.

Aaaah
opportunity!

Still
I wait till the next day
to call back the ad company.

"Look, I'd like you to take
my name out of the running
for this one.
OK?"

DO NOT READ THIS POEM

this poem eats paper and spits it out
it is part of the military industrial complex
no matter what is written
some of the money earned by this poem
is involved in insane forestry
depraved mining
it took food to make this poem
dentistry, nurturing
there had to be a house, a borning room
a butcher's shop
this poem and health care
plus pst plus gst
this poem and its plastic containers
many times cast off
there is no mask that can hold this poem
it is your see-through, walk-through
everything-is-what-it-appears-to-be poem
with no pretensions
utilitarian
as good as a sickle
as good as an electric chair
this poem torn from child-time
carved from moon-time
this poem that objects that things fall
that rails anyway
this poem that points the finger
at all of you
who point the finger

MORE TIME RELEASE POEMS

Though the candle is crooked
the flame is still straight
*

Sometimes the shadow is bigger
than the cat
*

If you change either
you change the other
*

Beware of the cautious
*

Be bold
or be bowled over
*

Everything leads
to everything else
*

You get bitter
and then you get better
*

Sometimes it is the book
that opens you
*

Are you ready for the euthanasia
YET?
*

There is no neck
like the head itself
*

Don't blame the mirror
for your face

*

I can't wait
to be patient

*

It is easiest to fast
just after eating

*

The knife will not soften
for the throat

*

The arrow is fastest
just before it strikes

*

Stop procrastinating
tomorrow!

*

There is nothing so efficient
as the last match

*

One tooth works with another

*

Every tooth affects the bite

*

Every turn of the wheel
sharpens the knife

*

Every little drop
makes the rain

*

If you want to bounce
you've got to hit the bottom

*

A fool will always find
banana skins

*

A fool cannot tell a pie
from a face cloth

*

No one is too stupid
to be a Fool

*

There is nothing to stop a fool
from becoming a high school teacher

*

There are fools even among the wise

*

A fool may live with a wise man
a thousand years and still know nothing

*

Maybe we've got nothing
but nothing lasts forever

*

You cannot avoid the void

*

You cannot refuse the rain

*

Are you ready for the euthanasia **YET?**

IN SLOW APOCALYPSE

MESSENGER

running past the black cities
their temples dark against the stars
they are insignia randomly cast
everything has some meaning
there are motifs in the windows
each rivulet reads like a possible gospel
there is so much to be imparted
but all is in code
let me by: I am running in my sacred duty
I have been scrawled upon by god
look, there are rhythms in my stride
full of powerful information — incantations
formulae, there are exquisite proofs of innocence
enscripted in my flesh
please read me
please decipher
this whipped soundscape of skin
put the stylus to my fingerwhorls
that the world might know my song

for they have cracked the code of the wind
in any given face
and they can now know the exact articulations of water
as it exhales itself against a palm —
your lips
all seem to be saying the same thing
please touch me
read this braille
surely there is some lost psalm in my flesh
please tell me what I say

INCARNATION

have a place for me
a perfect fit
make me one with my need
pour the warm light liquid
all down my naked body
i have a genetic expectation
a feeling for arrival
i'm coming down
like a thousand birds onto the black branch
i'm coming down
a zeppelin, a bag of blue air
into the tree-shaped brains
into the dendrite forest
into the longing cell
i have toes for my toes
and nose for my nose
i'm coming down into my liver
descending into my lungs
i am diving down into the cold
black waters of the belly
a million miles into my stomach
and i still have not rung
the bottom's deep belltone
i am drifting down in mind's vines
into clear blue bones
into the orange skull, the blind gristle
in pulses of pure black soul
through a long rubber tube
through a bronze body
on a reel
on an anchor long since sunk
in the never-to-be-shaken bottom of me
to the blackened tree
mind cross
joining place
to the socket

in the riverbed
the pierced Cartesian crossroad
with a stitch of uncuttable time
i am coming down
like the entire airforce
onto the black ship
i am coming down like the monarchs on Mexico

the body is a vast tropic
unreachable by foot
i am lost between volcanoes
there are a thousand miles of air
above my head
in a moment more
a second more
my feet will touch the ground
and my feet
are the ground
my eyes *are* the light
the air breathes me in
and exhales me in a long fluttering flow
i am down in my body
like the liquid rains
like the finally fallen peak
the obese suspended Buddhas
the plutonium Christs with their tears of heavy water
i am down with my jade-grown bones
my spirit legs bicycling
and the earth touches me
like a forever denied son
like an exile returned illegally
the earth touches me like a long lost mother
and her name is terra
terror
her name is life

POEM FOR RELUCTANT THREAD

yours is not to question
you are the thread not the tailor
you are the ship you are not the sailor
you must push yourself through
like a screwed up serviette through a donut hole
like a bag of beans through the effigy's eyes

all face
all piercing eyes
you must push yourself through
that's how you thread the needle
you give up your red reels of search unto the weaver
you surrender your long blue skein of yearning to the
   seamstress
all now shall be taken by the frayed brow
and pushed inaccurately into tight situations
you are getting a hand

how beautiful you will be in tapestry
what a moment of red your own pure red will make
in the autumns of red woven there
you would push yourself through for this
in long gulping strands
in gallops of green

you are such perfect thread
you are haute thread
but you will come to nothing
unless you submit
to the eye of the needle

THE REDRESS

When I finally told her she said: "Oh I'm so sorry." And her eyes seemed to cave in like depressions in the desert finally giving way to some underground abscess running inwards and away from me grain by grain in shame. "Oh I'm so sorry. I was so young and we didn't know any better and it wasn't like it is now. Back then the woman got nothing if she left the man and I couldn't have left you with him and I guess it was a cry for help." And my tears there in the afternoon in the old house. My tears like stones rolled from graves, like stones rolled from resurrection groves. And someone's knocked out a wall in my guts and 8 years of light, 8 years of childhood are glowing through my mother's hands right there, waving, pulling me in, tender before the fall.

DANIEL AGE 3

Daniel slips away
but he's still standing there
riding the blue wave
into a painting
into a story
or just a fantasy-thought
one more little cape
for identity to twirl in his
wild shaman's shuffle

O Dan who began with a smile
and then just smiled more

O Dan
who started with a laugh
and hit the highest note
I ever heard

PRAYER FOR MY SON

may your head be whole my son
despite the collision
may your great grey mind
still rest there clean upon the pages
you have loved so well
coming down like a beast to water
to read and loll there all day long
taking in Tolkien, Robert Jordan, Ursula LeGuin
all of them in long-abiding gulps, irritable to read
demanding to read
may your mind be well my son
it sits in the world like the top of a fuse
of miracle thought
amazing motion —
dances we will unwind and do
together and apart
I must ask to put my blessing at your feet
to help you keep them solidly upon this earth

it was me who caught the foot
and lifted it too high
to bring you crashing down
Hephaestus to the ground
O god! may your brow be well my son
my genius son

GRANDMOTHER

Goodbye grandmother
You were bigger than your life
You outlived the Thames and Walton
You outlived all the boys and men

You are old with novels grandmother
there are generations in this blue-veined skin
your old withered body a pulsing map
of what has been
what's come down
into the flesh
in this endless age
this age of credulity

Who made aeroplanes against the Kaiser
Who fed Canadian boys
in the Second World War
Who saw Queen Victoria's funeral barge
when she was two
go by her on the Thames

A drive that couldn't be turned off
even late into the nineties
when humbled by old age's
last instructive agonies
she could still do *Knees Up Mother Brown*
still play the piano
and flirt with young men

I shall never taste a mince pie so good
There will never be Christmasses so good
as those generous Christmasses
in your magnetic house
Thank you for those two rooms
from all four of us
Thank you for that first shelter here
in the frozen north

I can't believe
I will never see you
in this life
again

PRAYER FOR MY FRIENDS IN PAIN

may they last the night
my friends who are hurting badly
my friends in great agony
my friends who walk toward the bridge
may they last the night
for i know if they get through to the morning
they will have gone a long way into the agony
they will have gone so far into the agony
they will be coming out of it
they will be coming out of it

JACK THE INSOMNIAC

I am Jack the Insomniac — a kind of Rip Van Winkle in reverse — 20 years of insomnia is fine, but it is part of my gift that I do not accept the gift. I resist wakefulness. I can't help it, when everybody else goes to bed I get lonely. I want to go to bed too. In fact I am dying to sleep. I do all the rituals well — the walking in circles, the salutation to the sun, tense, efficient, now a hot bath stirred sideways, a brisk shit, a harried read and now to dread to bed yes, I get in the bed and I lie down and then I remember — the sleeping tea! I get up, head to the kitchen, prepare the tea and return to bed. Maybe the TV will help. There are talk shows on. These are sedative. Where's my Vicks? The tryptophan? I lie down finally and turn and click and switch and stick my head up one side and watch awhile like that. Then I click again till I think I must surely be getting tired. I lie flat now — the pillow under my neck. I take a deep breath, forgetting who I am, and think I'll just listen & click, not that, click not that, click. . .

It's been three nights now. I can feel a big ball of sleep submerged in my being, luxuriant enticing but impenetrable. Several times the ball wells up, overwhelming the little bit of mind, an image dancing, slides, I might just take this ticket but no, click, remember I am Jack the Insomniac. If I am not asleep by 2 I'll take the tryptophan. I can still sleep 4 hours, be up by 6 and my world is dancing, but I just missed that ticket. There is a small magnetic sound in the house and I remember. I need the fan on. I get up, creep in the other room where people are snoring, the lovely faces opaque with desire, destiny, inner alertness, comfort, dreams and without envy I remove the fan, take it down. Aaaah. That will probably do it. I lie back down. If I'm not asleep by 3 I'll take the tryptophan. Aaah the luxury of sleep. To live in instantly created environments tangent to the worry, the hassle, the domain, the plentitude of the sleepless one.

When will he accept that he is vibrating? When will he accept that his spine stands straight up above the bed like a divining rod to his soul shouting, "Son of water you are Jack the Insomniac"? I have danced in a lyrical way the world would love and just as I would come down skidding, madly sliding into sleep I slither, I scrape, I stop. There is a sound or a moment in the throat that draws me up again out of the fertile water, still hooked to the sharp curve of this night when I lost everything, gave up comfort, rhythm, vitality, to become a guardian, a watcher, a werewolf. My being vibrates between the two worlds. Some of it in some of it out. Bits going backward, bits being erased, bits not even making it to memory or moment at all. But they're all there and fucking awake anyway. I begin to pray: please god help me, please god let me sleep. I want to go upstairs and apologize to my children. I want to wake up my beloved and weep of my love for her. I am a much deeper being here. The wave has had to come up into this world to get me. A giant on the thin bed, this man who fell out of time, opiate-eyed but wide awake. What a blossoming to strip off the skins of sleep seven layers deep to enter this new life naked, but what I'd give to spread wide at last these two leaden wings of Insomnia and fall.

TRACKING HANDS

Hands dissolved in hands — a solution of hands, each hand a snowflake falling, losing its rage in a tear, melting off magic with a moment at the mouth of whatever denies things in me. Hey, these hands have fallen from me unseen in my autumn dream, a forest in the flesh — look deep roots in my eyes, of longing. But where there should be shelter — where there should be nature there is nothing, handless — nothing to take or to be received, just these battered things hung up and beaten by strange men. My hands, my brutal butchered hands. God, I threw away my prayer hands and wherever they go now, I feel it in my guts, strange works taking shape, strange caresses haunting me over the land. Who will forgive, who will knit into knuckles, my nail bitten hands? I will go the way they went. I will follow these disconnected bits. Where poems go. Where nasty letters go. Where there are prints in a child's flesh, bruises in a neck, or in tree trunks randomly slashed — Aaaaah my brutal hand went there. My wept for hand-self. My leaf-self, my need-self gone gripping, gone running after wrong things.

MEDIUM

just a hole
a portal
one rib in a long transit
just a part where
something goes through
its purpose to permit transgression
to be at once entrance exit
mouth and throat
small skin puncture
in the inner arm

the stomach
never to remain full
always peristalsis
the downward spirals
of digestion
to a point
out
of you

all this highway
that i am
a gulp at something
always going through me

neither the beginning
nor the end
of a swallow

ODE TO THE ASSHOLE

the asshole is the exclamation dot
dropped off at the bottom of you
an apertured lens
visible only in slang moments
a hairy asterisk

the finest
circle of instinct ever
elastic sensate
highly responsive
it holds us in and issues us
joins the inner and outer worlds
the true halo
organic wedding band
most of all it's home
to instinct, evolution
a kind of water well
from which all rings
move outward
up through shores
of grief and bone
to brow and brain

it lets wisdom in
and hot air out

but not too proud
nor too vulnerable
for the darkest possible tasks
this snake of devolution and decay
this period at the end of you
bottom crown
blow hole
starlip

radar and trumpet
this peaceful
thoughtful
anus

POST-MODERN PENIS

in its cowl
like a monk
its head hung over
in humility

like a bloodhound
half up
out of the docket
nose high
with the first thick scent
of some right woman

neglected, hung up like
your mother's old coat
on a hook
for a month
unwashed
the stains still on it

another mind
supernaturally smart
another
wrinkled heart

half-hard
arched down — the eye slit
just leering out
from it prepuce patch
up periscope

the bathing penis
high in its crow's nest
buffoon-like
twirled clown
stupid root pig bit
stunted arm blood balloon

testicle companion
testicle exclamation
sinking in bit
delivering bit
with its backbone up
with its fine etched veins
pulsing visible in sex juice
this divining bone
manpart, heartroot
this hung cheese
this hung hog
in a butcher's shop
this disobedient flaccid dog
in its too-big suit
in its wrinkled robes
old patriarch
flung down
by god
sacred king
hanged man
tiddlybit
pee pee

tiniest tube
in the big
bone
world

ABOUT THE CREATION OF LIFE ON EARTH

What might be a merely technical experience in some species is, in the earthling, a beautiful ritual, written extempore, always in deep delphic tones, rivalling the euphonies of any nation's most sacred texts. And yet, as I say, the humans just spout this stuff. It is like breath to them. They inhale and exhale pure language at these times and no one can stop them as they speak, sing, sigh at one another just weaving in the attachments, drawing closer, first to lips to taste, I guess, the deeper information of wet mouth and tongue. And there are lingering assessments of breasts, chests, bellies. All are taken in, and even here the mate might just deposit some fertile spermatazoa and be done but prior to the planting of the little seed in the big seed there is this dalliance with the pod. The pod that pouts and decorates itself with soft downs and springy turfs. The pod that only accurate individuated caresses can attempt to open naturally, wet with its own desire. Remember these are very sensitive parts. There are billions of receptors per square centimetre. More than some of us have in our entire beings. But these creatures have that many receptors in just the liquid rubbing part of themselves. So here it begins. The real uniqueness of earthly mating. For now the one with the little seeds, puts his bomb-topped stamen just at the lips of the one with the bigger seed and slowly she swallows him. He wedges into her. They are both partly liquid at this point. The most slippery and star-filtered parts of them are resolved into an instantly blissful oneness. This is beyond what we call touch. Two minds are meeting here. Two entire sensualities intersect accurately and ecstatically. This should be it, but I tell you the wonder deepens — the long bomb-headed stamen slides into the grasping gullet of the seed pod and sometimes here the legs will spread, buckle, tremble, embrace the full thrust of the delivering one. There are sounds arising now. Similarly tinged with this oneness, this starriness so rare in our species. But it is not just that the stamen must descend in this velvet tunnel to its deepest extremity and then extrude its fine human seed storm. No. There is a retreat. A withdrawal. A re-entry. Indeed this is but the first of a great number of forays, back and almost out, then slowly deeply back in. And out. Only to be slid in again deep, then out in and down: the pelvic bones yawning to swallow one another, all to stoke the head of the stamen, the hanging testicles where fathoms of the seed like feathers in a calm must be aroused by this holy rhythm till a small wind lifts them. Under guidance from the egg, these seeds are gently lifted. They are pushed up into the blue sensate skies, touching, softly, every part of the mind, until the stoking is complete and from beyond the feet, from outside this universe a force rushes in all through the bones and circuits to meet and melt here into matter, into seed, into storm and throng, pulse dust blow, the seed is propelled out in liquid moonstone, in strands of stardust. To head for the egg, the egg which has been sending signals all along. Waiting for the one or two to choose. To say which one is the one.

OUR SPIRITS ARE TRYING TO GET AT ONE ANOTHER

Our spirits are trying to get at one another
they want to get through
but what is this flesh in the way —
kiss it off, touch it off
open into it with a tongue
rub and writhe away this hot veil of skin on skin
and we shall get through
we shall get into one another

But we are moths in separate bottles, flap
flapping at the bright glass
as we pass by one another
with wide waving hands

Until we've melted through
we've fallen through another layer
and we still have skin
but our spirits are much closer now
yes, spirit has busted the dams and flooded the flesh
and now mutual ravens, butterflies, vultures
we pick at one another's tasty bits
lips, hips
in between the fingers
we are ants on ants and bees in bees
two honeycombs finally flowing,
all our colours have leaked out
my red, your blue
we're so mixed up in lavender kisses
it's hard to know who's who

SOME VERY GOOD REASONS WHY

because it had roses caught up in it
beautiful jade roses
because of green eyes whirling
i married the tornado
because i live on the edge
ever running
and i loved the tug
the slow revolving
of the seasons round her
and the house she had captured
in her still centre
the house where the world whirled

because of complete surrender
because of cunt juice and roses
i married into
the long genealogy of the whirlwind
just for a spin
just for the centrifugal force
i wanted the blood to move to my back

i keep far from the centre of a woman
i ride the edge
she was right for me
for she could lay me down like a prairie
and soothe my miles and meadows
because she threw herself on my mountains
absorbing all my seas, my upheavals, my neural moons
she was sick of taking on the world
why not just one man
suck up his heart
his poems into her still centre
and just stand like that
wild inside
still inside
ever over kansas
ever under oz

SAFE RAGE WITH MATES

You have to direct your anger at the action
not the person.
You can say:
Your actions really anger me.
But you can't say:
You make me really fucking mad.
The words **you make** are incorrect.
They place you in the passive "done-to" stance.
The above statement should be reworded:
I get really fucking mad around (or at) you.

This pigpen in the kitchen makes me really angry
however, is an open statement.
It might still be you who allowed
the alleged pigpen to occur.
But don't curse — **Pig!** — under your breath
for this is to the person and offensive.
Why can't we communicate is not offensive
but so negative
so void of potential.
There must be potential even in safe rage.

I am really angry and I need to talk to you
is not a good enticement.
You should not yell —
That's not yelling — THIS IS YELLING!
If you have to yell
you must yell something non-threatening like
Don't be scared. I am only yelling.
It is very important not to make a fist.

As a bottom line
when the only words your rage supplies
are race/gender slurs, or suicide threats,
it is currently deemed preferable and correct
to fall to the floor
and just shriek inarticulately.

A person shrieking on the floor inarticulately
has time out
the floor is a safe zone
the floor is off limits
and remember,
you must not
bare your teeth.

THERE IS NO SILENCE

there is no silence
like this silence
we break with sounds
we shouldn't make
sounds addictive
once begun
begun again
and again
in full veins
the tug or tremble
rush of blood
as the rhythm quickens
in smooth contact
the sounds of skin
of tongues
two tongues
there is no silence
like this soft silence
when the last sigh is done
and the tissues succumb
to their essential sensual quietness
only then
do we hear again
this pounding
this singing
this holiness
we once
thought
was one
heart

IT IS NOT LOVE AT FIRST SIGHT

it is not love at first sight
that is the miracle
it is love at ninth sight
love at the end of the night
it is love the next morning
that is the miracle

POEM YOU CAN'T REFUSE

here it comes
with grim warnings
and a head full of fallen trees
grinding out the old execution vowel
gushing the blues, twisting into the welcome silence
like a corkscrew through flesh —
the poem you can't refuse

you think you shouldn't have this poem
you've been warned about poems like this
but it's just so full of juice
just so tasty
and it's just standing there
with charcoal eyes beckoning you
like a dream come true
saying come and pay a few dues
come and lay your body down
in the poem you can't refuse

this poem has stalked you for so long
it saw you at your birth and watched you from afar
this poem has walked many streets beside you
always closing the distance
on a certain time
a certain place
one of a million poems
you could possibly choose
but this poem is different
it's the poem you can't refuse

with its mish-mash of mouth sounds
with its syllables borrowed from death
it's at your gates with hope songs
carbonated melodies
in great draughts of liquid language
effervescent in the soul
a child's bubble
a priest's prayer
some fool is babbling
in lost lingos
this dream talk
this karma tune
that plays out the long voice
of what you have to do
in your time on earth
it's life it's life it's life itself
the poem you can't refuse

IN SLOW APOCALYPSE

I love our moment in slow apocalypse
stretching out time
with tenderness or touch
and we speak fast here
in this crammed era
grateful for distortion
for digital
for the Doppler Effect

just before the fall
the dance is most intense —
a million moves a minute
scurrying to do
last things
meaning to build
more boats
grab someone and hold them close

rear back against the drift of images
let love flow against the age
offer our resistance
even in the detonator's mouth
we sing, we burn
to turn as slowly as possible
into fire and ashes

o raise a glass
to the flash
of slow apocalypse

WE RODE THE WORD

we rode the word then
it was our wild hog
our highway
and we rode it
habitually
always breaking into a new word
or exiting the old
we were never outside the word
or off the word
it was truly our magic white dust
it made us insane with power
with illusion
we thought we had potent magic
in these sounds
upon the page
god we didn't care what whizzed by
in the landscape
on the shore
our clutch, our possession
was the word
that no one else could get at
this skid into lingo
whether we got messed up or not
whether we got acknowledgement or not
we did not put away funds
just so long as there was language —
a mother tongue
a grease smear into lyric possibility
an escaped and fabulous beast
with us
on
it

WOMEN LOOKING BETTER LONGER

more and more women are looking gorgeous
and I thank the divine that I'm alive
in a time when women are looking so great
at a later age:
an age when 70-year-old women
look good to me; when 40-year-old women
make my lips ache
what lucky fools we are
to inhabit this century of attitude
when all those great faces of adolescence
are with us still, only foxier now,
that gold glint of life in their eyes,
that well done alcohol
of long-time sensuality
there is nothing youth has
that can get you that — only life
and there is such life in them
I want to look in and drink it all
singing Alleluiah —
women looking better longer
women looking amazing at a later and later age
whatever else we've done
by grace or nature
by voodoo or brush
by cream or steam
we've done well here
'cause more and more people are beautiful and strong
and we're just going to have to adjust —
deal with the beauty
learn not to stare, not to swoon
not to blush and gurgle

because it's not just exteriors
it's not just mystery
it's just that she
the beloved
evolves toward something
I love the look of

THIS LIFE I'M SUPPOSED . . .

This life I'm supposed to learn
something about a beautiful face
I'm supposed to remember that I'm not here
just to pay old dues
I'm here at the opening in my life
silver sun coming in from everywhere
and I have the power to tap this light
run with it or be riven by it
me, just one of its solubles standing up

They say that I have been created
by a field of information
before identity
a set of infinite possibilities

Aaaaaah
that explains it

But they keep shoving beautiful faces in my face
and I'm getting good at checking with myself
saying, hang on now . . . give it oh, maybe six
or seven very sweet nights
and then you'll get to the big box of lures
the ragged old-time complexities
the catch at the lip

No there are some kisses too sweet for life itself
to contain at a material level
kisses that spill over into spirit stuff
so what am I supposed to do?

Continue to reason
or just wash it all through
with some very nice whisky?

A fool for sugar
a man born to fall into flowers
and get stuck there
a honey addict
just wants to saturate his wings with the feminine
to widen the glint of silver in some eyes
till it takes you in and radiates every cell
so that a face — a possibility
can dissolve time
and you stand there in the field
radiant, hypnotic, pure soul

TRANSFORMER

i was good at being the poor man
i did the beaten man well
i lingered with the poor boy
the boy with a bad father
i was good as the boy with the bad father
i did it
and i did it
and i did it
there were things i almost became —
angels, accidents, birds mostly
but sometimes stone
and once light

once light — forever light!
i lingered on the light
i wanted to be light always
but i had to be the neonate
the soul seed zygote blastocyst
i was bad at being a baby
stunned at the beauty and intensity of having nerves
receptors everywhere — light in the heavy place
coming in off everything
need too — need!

i still dream of being the falling man
though i have never fallen
i loved being Christ, naked on the cross
i loved being Kennedy
with the big chunk flying
i loved being Lennon — my heart opened
from behind
by assassin's bullets

some transformations i don't quite make —
bits of me stuck evolving —
my hands less evolved than my feet
my feet the extremities of a saint
with holy arches and long toes
i've been yanking at my limbs for some time now
trying to be complete —
Buddha — the wise one
but i keep collapsing into an ass
a laughing stock

i hate the dying part of it
i hate the remembering and regretting
i like the part where the broad light
erupts from the narrow filament in my belly
and the soul opens like a senseless trumpet lily
to be played by that force

all too briefly

i am flame
foam, fly in light
i am spirit stuff
water reflecting one sun
a thousand times
each ripple ecstatic
with its own distortion
of the one
i want to be
the one

FIXING THE SEED

The man had the seed a long time
but he could not get it to grow
so he took the seed to a doctor
and the doctor advised an operation
he took the seed to a priest
and the priest advised prayer
the psychotherapist suggested meditation —
rumination on the seed's as-yet uncovered past
but the seed wouldn't grow
faith healers danced and did the mambo
but produced not the tiniest swelling
on the seed's sullen surface

The man tried always being with the seed
then he tried always leaving the seed alone
he tried talking to the seed
singing to it
but there was no change
the seed would not grow

A monk chanted over the seed's crowned head
there were healing circles
seances
treatments with magnets, needles
there were rituals
sacrifice
imaging

"I see the seed growing," the man said
but the seed did not grow
the seed was dead

So they called in a resurrectionist
for a laying on of hands
but the seed could not be resurrected
nothing anyone said or did
produced the tiniest twinge of a sprout
in that poor dead seed

The man was old by now and tired
this loss was a terrible bitterness
on his tongue

Singing
keening a grief
he prepared a small place
in the ground for the seed
and with some ceremony
placed it there softly
covering it over with soil
dead

Dead
he wept
and just so
the seed began to grow

- Cap-Saint-Ignace
- Sainte-Marie (Beauce)
Québec, Canada
1997